Level 5
TECHNIQUE
Exploring Piano Classics
A Masterwork Method for the Developing Pianist

NANCY BACHUS

Alfred Music Publishing Co., Inc.
P.O. Box 10003
Van Nuys, CA 91410-0003
alfred.com

ISBN-10: 0-7390-8484-4
ISBN-13: 978-0-7390-8484-7

About the *Exploring Piano Classics*

Exploring Piano Classics: A Masterworks Method for Developing Pianists pairs performance repertoire with related technical studies. Each level contains two books:

■ *Exploring Piano Classics—Repertoire* includes pieces from the major style periods. The repertoire was selected and graded from festival, competition, and examination lists from the United States (MTNA), Canada (RCM), and the United Kingdom (ABRSM). Background information on each style period, its instruments, composers, and the music itself is included. The CD performances of the repertoire are an indispensable tool for motivation and for modeling stylistic interpretations.

■ *Exploring Piano Classics—Technique* includes **basic keyboard patterns**—five-finger patterns, scales, chords, cadences, and arpeggios in the major and minor keys of the literature in the *Repertoire* book of the same level. These patterns can be developed into a daily warm-up routine for each practice session; through gradual progression in difficulty, a solid technical foundation is built.

These companion books are cross-referenced, enabling quick access to the correlating repertoire or technical study. This allows the teacher to assign pages in the *Technique* book that directly apply to the pieces students are learning in the *Repertoire* book.

About the Technique Books

Technique is a skill that can be developed by both athletes and pianists. Both fields require practice of desired skills until automatic, and then they can be used successfully in performances. A well-functioning piano technique is effortless, comfortable, and pain-free. (Pianists should never play with pain.) *Exploring Piano Classics* suggests physical motions and sensations to encourage students to experiment with different muscle groups to discover how to play in a way that feels natural, easy, and comfortable.

Each new level of *Exploring Piano Classics* builds on the previous levels while adding new technical patterns and skills necessary to play the advancing repertoire. *Technique*, Level 5, emphasizes **voicing and developing velocity/speed in a variety of keys**. Etudes are an essential part of pianists' training, and the ones selected (from the thousands available) directly relate to *Repertoire*, Level 5.

Technique, Level 5, has more **etudes** than previous levels to help students in the application of the basic technical patterns (scales, chords, etc.) to repertoire. Etudes routinely repeat a particular pattern or challenge several times, enabling mastery, while repertoire requires more rapid changes in patterns and motions.

Working through the *Technique* books will give students a structured program of technical development—a technical foundation that will enable them to progress to higher levels—to play skillfully and musically throughout their lives.

CONTENTS

Arches in the Hand

An **arch** is a **curved structure** over a space that is also a **support** (for a bridge, building, etc.).

The **keystone** locks and holds the arch together.

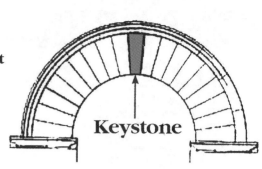

Keystone

In piano playing:

■ An arch is created in the palm **between the knuckles of fingers 1 and 5** (see Arch 1).

The **knuckles of fingers 2 and 3** act as the **keystone** of the arch between fingers 1 and 5, supporting the relaxed weight of the arm on the fingertips.

■ The energy from **finger 1** (thumb) creates an arch to the **knuckle** of finger 2 (see Arch 2).

■ This arch **connects** finger 1 with the other fingers. The forearm and elbow help support the hand and fingertips on the keyboard. It feels like a slightly lifted (arched) **ramp** or bridge **under the forearm** to the palm (see Arch 3).

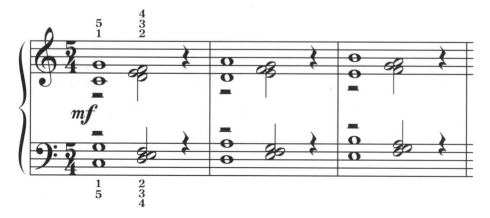

Arches Exercise

In each measure, in rhythm:

■ Beat 1: **Fall** on fingers 1 and 5, aiming energy toward the knuckles.

■ Beat 2: Make a **scratching motion** on the keys with fingers 1 and 5, **creating an arch** with the palm muscles.

■ Beat 3: Play fingers 2-3-4 together to **create another arch** between fingers 1 and 2 while still holding fingers 1 and 5.

■ Beat 4: **Direct energy to the knuckles** of fingers 2 and 3 (**keystone**) for strong arches. Feel a ramp-like arch under the forearm, which is lifted, not pushed down.

■ Beat 5: Fingers 2-3-4 slightly **pull the forearm forward** as keys are released.

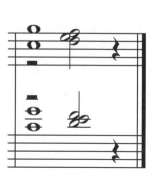

continue
upward
until...

Five-Finger Review

When playing five-finger patterns, maintain the arches in the hands, feeling a continuous **legato connection** in the knuckles and fingertips.

Repeat each measure of *Little Pischna No. 1* **three times**. When comfortable with the pattern, **vary the touches**:

- Play as written with **LH legato**, then with **LH staccato**.

- Also, **double the tempo** with **both hands legato**.

Little Pischna No. 1

Johann Pischna (1826–1896)
Bernhard Wolff (1835–1906)

6

Repeat each measure of *Little Pischna No. 3* **three times**. When comfortable with the pattern, **vary the touches**:

▪ Play as written with **RH legato**, then with **RH staccato**.

▪ Also, **double the tempo** with **both hands legato**.

Little Pischna No. 3

Johann Pischna (1826-1896)
Bernhard Wolff (1835-1906)

Voicing: The Divided Hand

Voicing in piano music refers to the way **lines are balanced**. In orchestras and choirs, different instruments or singers are given various parts while pianists must show the separate lines (or voices) through contrast in **dynamics and tone colors**.

Voicing requires that individual fingers of the same hand perform separate tasks, such as one finger holding down a key while other fingers play.

- It may be helpful to think of each hand as having an **outer hand** (fingers 3-4-5) and an **inner hand** (fingers 1-2-3).

- **Finger 3** helps direct the weight to either side of the hand.

Finger 3 weighting the **outer hand** (fingers 3-4-5)

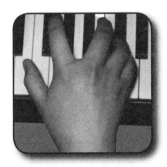

Finger 3 weighting the **inner hand** (fingers 1-2-3)

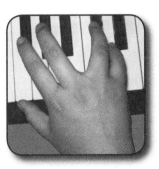

Play the **top voice as legato as possible** and the other voices **detached**. Direct weight to the RH **outer hand**.

Voicing Exercise

Trills and Mordents

The most common ornaments found in Baroque era music are the **mordent** and the **trill**. Both are played rhythmically **on the beat**.

In the following exercises:

- Play slowly with precise fingertip action, keeping **the thumb joint at the wrist loose**.

- Gradually increase speed until playing the ornaments in **one motion of the arm**.

- Practice **different finger combinations**, and also with the **LH one octave lower** than written.

Baroque **trills** usually **begin on the note above the written note** and have at least **four notes** (or more if the ornamented note is longer).

The Short Trill

William Mason
(1829-1908)

Mordents usually **begin on the written note** and contain **three notes**.

The Mordent

William Mason
(1829-1908)

	Common Articulations (Touches) in Baroque and Classical Styles	
Touch	**Notation**	**How Performed**
Legato	slur mark	connected smoothly and continuously
	slur groups	legato groups with a graceful release carried on one motion of the arm
Staccato	dots or wedges	short, bouncy sounds; wedge is shorter than dot
Non-Legato or Portato	unmarked or both slurred and staccato	detached sounds; semi-legato or long staccato

Warm-Up Patterns in C

Using a metronome to maintain a steady ♩ pulse:

■ Play the Parallel Motion scale first ♩ one octave, then ♫ two octaves, then ♫♩ three octaves, and then ♬ four octaves.

C Major Scales in Progressive Rhythms

■ Play the Combined Parallel and Contrary Motion scale as written.

Chord Progression and Variations in C

■ Play the *Chord Progression and Variations in C* as written in major, and repeat in minor by lowering all E's and A's a half step.

■ **Relax** the wrist and knuckles after striking each chord, keeping the nail joints firm.

Blocked chord

■ **Balance** on the half notes, keeping the weight constant.

Divided chord

■ Maintain the **arch** connection between fingers 1 and 4 or 5.

Alberti bass

■ Use a **throwing motion** to group four eighth notes in one forward motion.

Divided chord pattern

Dominant Seventh Chords in C (Broken and Blocked)

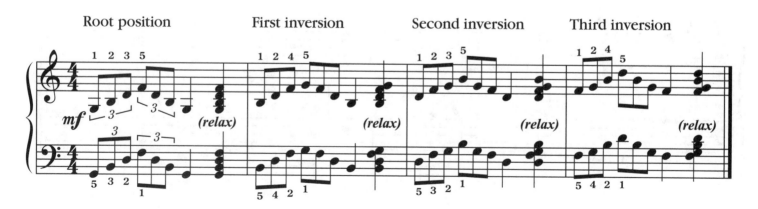

Repeat in minor by lowering all E's a half step.

Broken Chords and Inversions

- First play hands separately in ♩ rhythm. Repeat as written in ♫ rhythm.

- Align the forearm with finger 3 to begin. Lightly touch the elbow (with other hand) to keep it stationery, allowing the **wrist to pivot** as the **forearm aligns** with the finger that is playing.

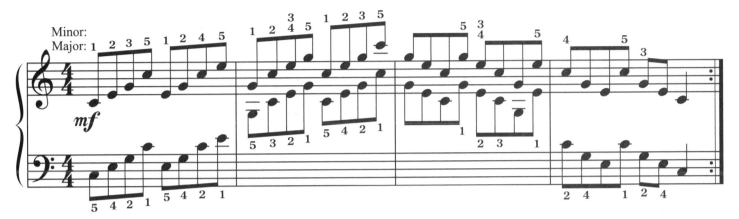

Arpeggio Prep

- Move the **forearm** in a continuous **horizontal motion**, parallel to the keyboard.

- **Avoid turning the wrist**, and keep the upper arm relaxed.

This

Forearm moving horizontally (RH)

Not This

Wrist is turned (RH)

Arpeggio Exercise in C

- **Keeping the hand shape**, use a continuous forearm motion, without turning the wrist.

Hearing Two Voices

Within a single line certain **notes** may be **more important than others**.
In *Rotation Exercises*, play the moving lines (eighth-note rhythm) more prominently.

■ First practice with **alternating hands** playing the moving line *mf* with one hand and the repeated notes *p* with the other one.

■ Then, with **one hand**, play the moving lines **legato** and repeated notes **staccato**.

Rotation Exercise
(Right Hand)

Carl Czerny (1791–1857)
Op. 261, No. 5

Rotation Exercise
(Left Hand)

Carl Czerny (1791–1857)
Op. 261, No. 6

Scale Forms in C Minor

Using a metronome to maintain a steady ♩ pulse:

■ Play each scale first ♩ one octave, then ♫ two octaves, then ♫♩ three octaves, and then ♬ four octaves.

C Minor Scales

C Natural Minor uses the key signature.

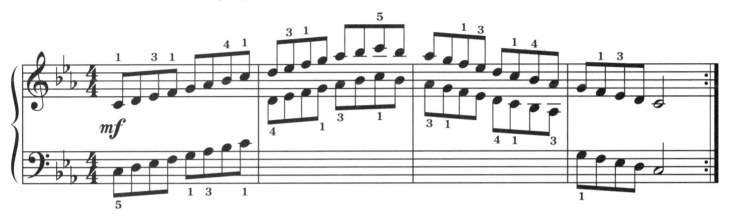

C Harmonic Minor uses the key signature with the 7th scale degree raised a half step.

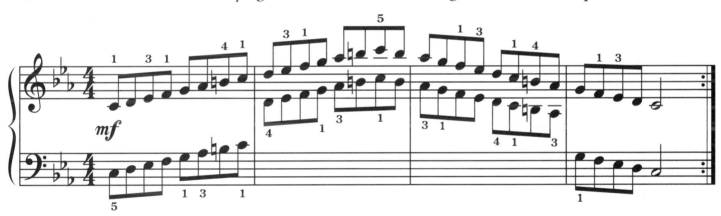

C Melodic Minor uses the key signature with the 6th **and** 7th scale degrees raised a half step ascending; uses only the key signature descending (the natural minor scale).

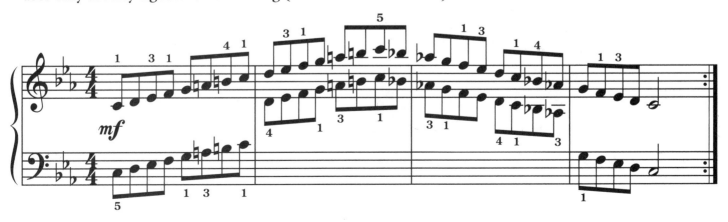

Voicing: Imitation

When a musical idea is repeated in a different hand or voice, it is known as **imitation**. Both lines in the following example have two-note slurs and should be played with **similar dynamics and character**.

▦ The first note of each slur group should have a **gentle emphasis** with no lift between groups.

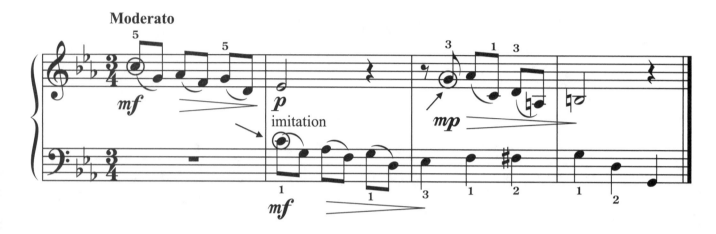

Voicing: Multiple Voices

Several lines played together should first be **practiced separately** to gain control of the dynamics. Practice as follows in the example below:

▦ First, sustain the dotted-half notes in the bass. Keep the **weight constant** on G when adding the slurred quarter notes in both hands, playing them as a duet.

▦ In the eighth-note line, play the repeated **G's softer** than the moving B-naturals and C's (circled) since those G's are less important than the moving line.

▦ Finally, **echo** the repetition (by bringing palm close to keyboard) when playing all the lines.

Warm-Up Patterns in G

Using a metronome to maintain a steady ♩ pulse:

■ Play the Parallel Motion scale first ♩ one octave, then ♫ two octaves, then ♪♪♪ three octaves, and then ♬♬ four octaves.

G Major Scales in Progressive Rhythms

Parallel Motion

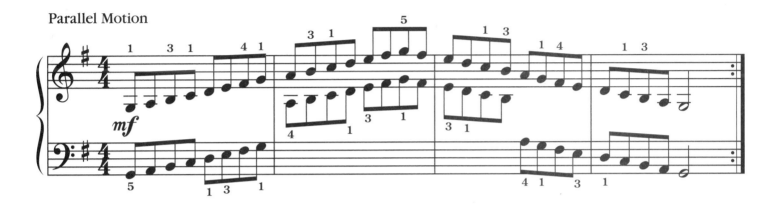

■ Play the Combined Parallel and Contrary Motion scale as written.

Combined Parallel and Contrary Motion

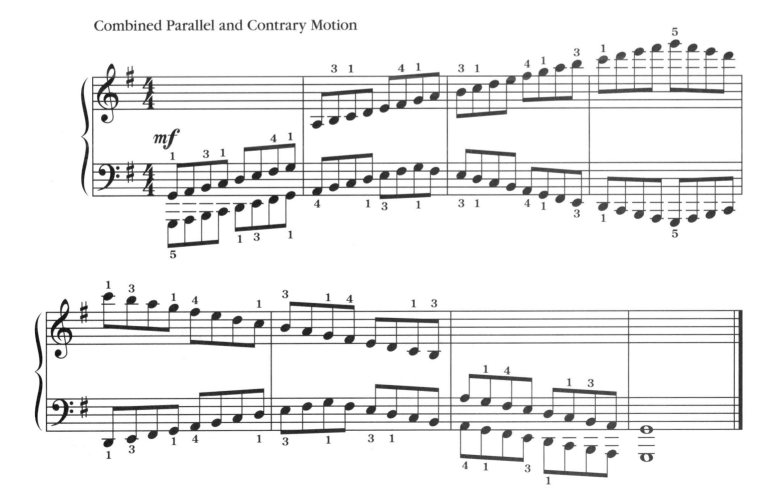

Chord Progression and Variations in G

■ Play the *Chord Progression and Variations in G* as written in major, and repeat in minor by lowering all B's and E's a half step.

■ **Relax** the wrist and knuckles after striking each chord, keeping the nail joints firm.

Blocked chord

■ **Balance** on the half notes, keeping the weight constant.

Divided chord

■ Maintain the **arch** connection between fingers 1 and 4 or 5.

Alberti bass

■ Use a **throwing motion** to group four eighth notes in one forward motion.

Divided chord pattern

Dominant Seventh Chords in G (Broken and Blocked)

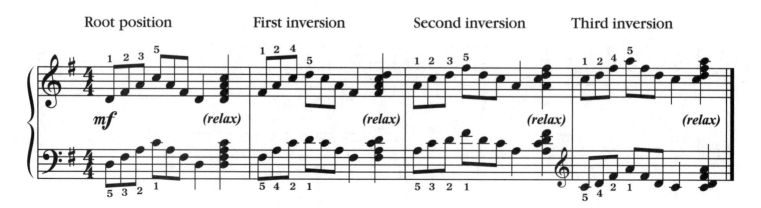

Repeat in minor by lowering all B's a half step.

Broken Chords and Inversions

■ First play hands separately in ♩ rhythm. Repeat as written in ♫ rhythm.

■ Align the forearm with finger 3 to begin. Lightly touch the elbow (with other hand) to keep it stationery, allowing the **wrist to pivot** as the **forearm aligns** with the finger that is playing.

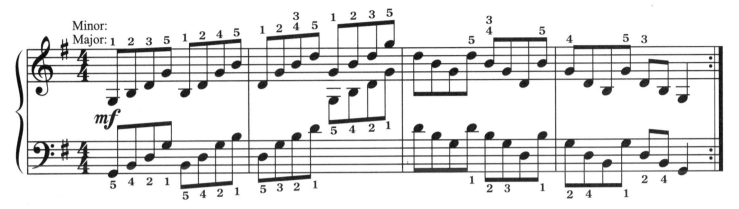

Arpeggio Prep

■ **Balance on finger 1** after it crosses under.

■ Do not let finger 1 collapse or turn the wrist.

This

Finger 1 balanced

Not This

Finger 1 collapsed

Arpeggio Exercise in G

■ **Keeping the hand shape**, use a continuous forearm motion, without turning the wrist.

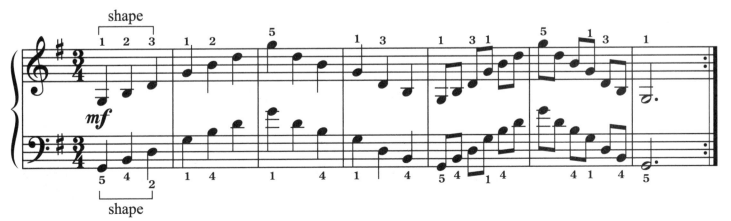

On the Lake, p. 10

Cantabile ("Singing") Melodies

Melodies need a **penetrating tone** and should be "shaped" as a singer would sing them.

- Singers usually crescendo when holding longer notes.

- On the piano, longer notes naturally diminuendo (or decay) when held.

- When playing a melody, listen carefully to what remains of a longer note, and play the following note as softly as necessary to make a smooth, continuous line.

Crossing Over the Left-Hand Thumb

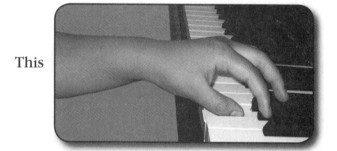

This

Move the forearm horizontally when crossing over finger 1 in the LH.

Not This

Do not turn the wrist or kick up the elbow.

Arpeggio Etude
(Excerpt)

Jean-Baptiste Duvernoy (1802–1880)
Op. 120, No. 7

Scale Forms in G Minor

Using a metronome to maintain a steady ♩ pulse:

▪ Play each scale first ♩ one octave, then ♫ two octaves, then ♪♪♪ three octaves, and then ♬ four octaves.

G Minor Scales

G Natural Minor uses the key signature.

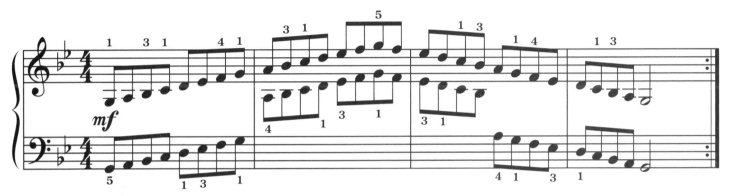

G Harmonic Minor uses the key signature with the 7th scale degree raised a half step.

G Melodic Minor uses the key signature with the 6th **and** 7th scale degrees raised a half step ascending; uses only the key signature descending (the natural minor scale).

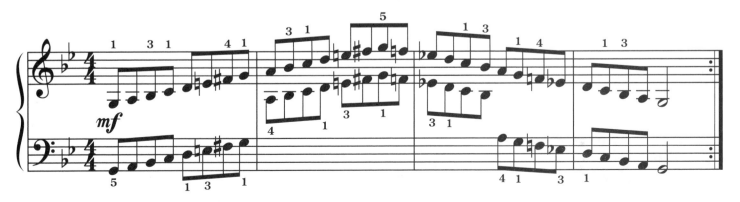

Berceuse, p. 12

Imitation: Cantabile ("Singing") Motives

Imitation, when similar motives are repeated in the other hand, must be clear to listeners.

- Play each motive with **one motion**, feeling the weight shift from fingertip to fingertip.

- **Relax** the forearm to help the **crescendo**.

- The following excerpt from Henri Bertini was originally in G major.

Follow Me
(Excerpt)

Henri Bertini (1798–1876)
Op. 100, No. 14
Arr. Nancy Bachus

Velocity (Speed) in G Major

Many composers have written **velocity studies** for piano students, to increase their ability to move around the keyboard with ease and speed.

- Begin at a comfortable metronome speed, and then increase it by four points until difficult. Continue this for several days until reaching the speed you desire.

- Use more or less energy in the fingers to **increase** (as lines ascend) or **decrease** (as lines descend) dynamics. **Listen** to give the highest notes the most volume and the lowest the least.

- Move the arm in a **smooth continuous motion** for each line.

Speeding in G Major
(Excerpt from *School of Velocity*)

Cornelius Gurlitt (1820–1901)
Op. 141, No. 22

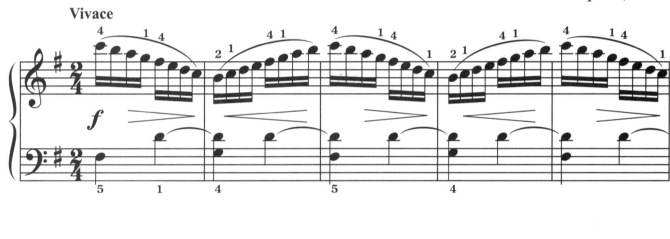

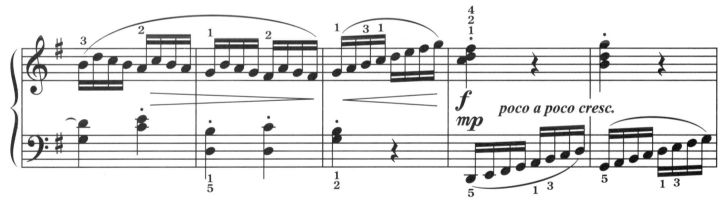

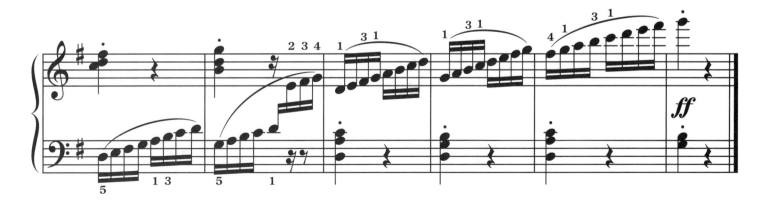

Warm-Up Patterns in D

Using a metronome to maintain a steady ♩ pulse:

■ Play the Parallel Motion scale first ♩ one octave, then ♫ two octaves, then ♫♫ three octaves, and then ♬ four octaves.

D Major Scales in Progressive Rhythms

Parallel Motion

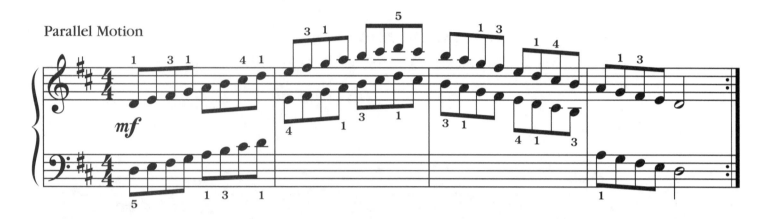

■ Play the Combined Parallel and Contrary Motion scale as written.

Combined Parallel and Contrary Motion

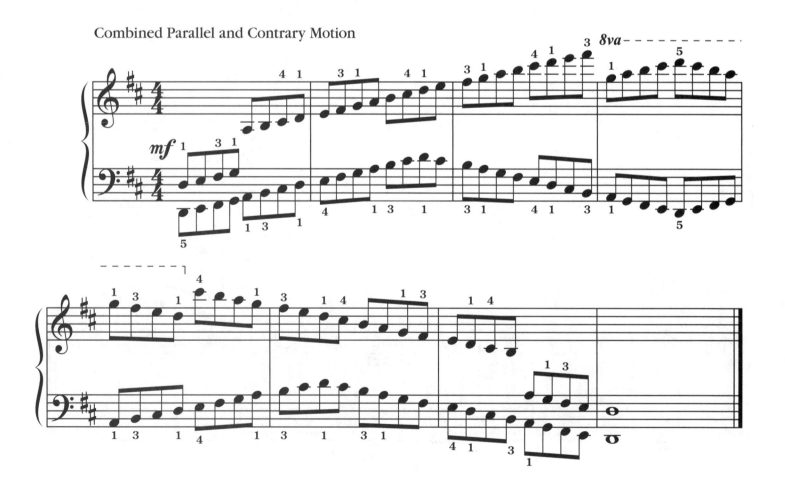

Chord Progression and Variations in D

■ Play the *Chord Progression and Variations in D* as written in major, and repeat in minor by lowering all F's and B's a half step.

■ **Relax** the wrist and knuckles after striking each chord, keeping the nail joints firm.

Blocked chord

■ **Balance** on the half notes, keeping the weight constant.

Divided chord

■ Maintain the **arch** connection between fingers 1 and 4 or 5.

Alberti bass

■ Use a **throwing motion** to group four eighth notes in one forward motion.

Divided chord pattern

Dominant Seventh Chords in D (Broken and Blocked)

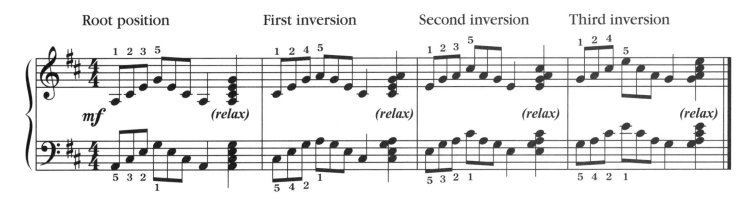

24

Repeat in minor by lowering all F's a half step.

Broken Chords and Inversions

- First play hands separately in ♩ rhythm. Repeat as written in ♫ rhythm.

- Align the forearm with finger 3 to begin. Lightly touch the elbow (with other hand) to keep it stationery, allowing the **wrist to pivot** as the **forearm aligns** with the finger that is playing.

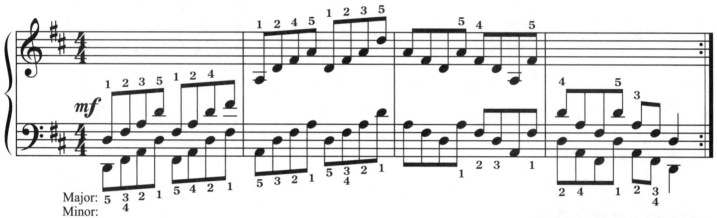

Arpeggio Prep

- Move the **forearm** in a smooth **horizontal motion** as finger 1 crosses under the hand.

- **Do not turn the wrist** as finger 1 crosses under the hand.

This

Forearm moving horizontally (LH)

Not This

Wrist is turned (LH)

Arpeggio Exercise in D

- **Keeping the hand shape**, use a continuous forearm motion, without turning the wrist.

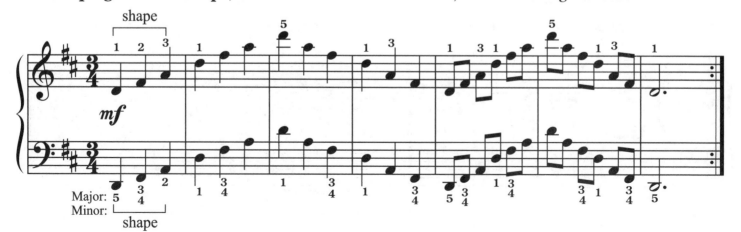

Moving Smoothly in D Major

First, play the ♩. notes legato. Use **finger substitution** in measure 3 to connect the dotted-half notes seamlessly.

LH Voicing Exercise:

To move quickly around the keyboard in the key of D major:

■ The angle of finger 1 must **maintain its arch** with finger 2. Make a U-shape, not a V-shape, between fingers 1 and 2.

■ **Balance** on the **angled** finger 1 as the forearm and hand move sideways as a unit:

U-shaped arch

Racing in D Major

Jean-Baptiste Duvernoy (1802–1880)
Op. 176, No. 9

Scale Forms in D Minor

Using a metronome to maintain a steady ♩ pulse:

■ Play each scale first ♩ one octave, then ♫ two octaves, then ♪♪♪ three octaves, and then ♬ four octaves.

D Minor Scales

D Natural Minor uses the key signature.

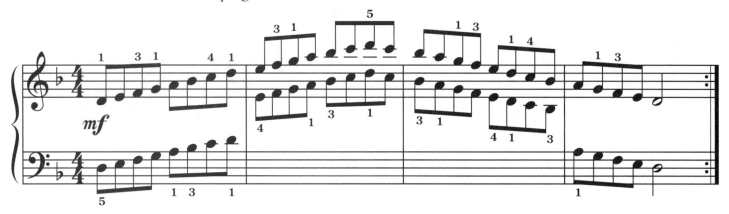

D Harmonic Minor uses the key signature with the 7th scale degree raised a half step.

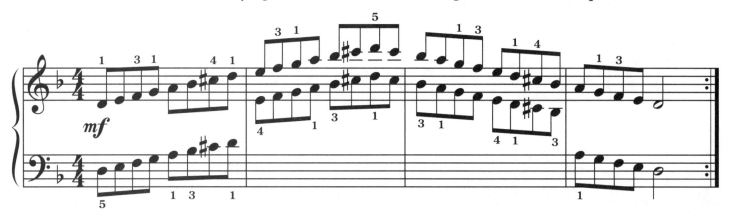

D Melodic Minor uses the key signature with the 6th **and** 7th scale degrees raised a half step ascending; uses only the key signature descending (the natural minor scale).

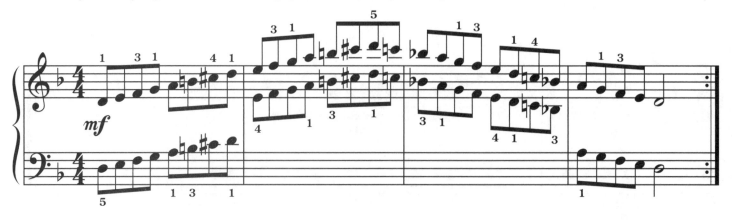

Alternating Touches

Many different touches and motions are used to play the piano.

- **Scale passages** need **smooth horizontal motions** of the arm to help carry the fingers.

- To group **repeated chords**, use one **forward throwing motion** from the upper arm for each measure. Fingers should remain on the keys.

- **Slurs** are played in one motion: **fall—connect—release**.

Practice each motion until comfortable.

Allegretto in D Minor

Arnoldo Sartorio (1853–1936)
Arr. Nancy Bachus

Balancing Melody and Repeated Chords

Repeated notes and chords require careful listening on the piano because there will be a crescendo created by the repetition. **Begin repeated notes softly** and listen for dynamic control.

When repeated notes are in an inner voice, keep the **weight constant on the outer notes**. Use **finger substitution** to make a continuous legato.

Voicing Warm-Up (from Op. 141, No. 8, Cornelius Gurlitt)

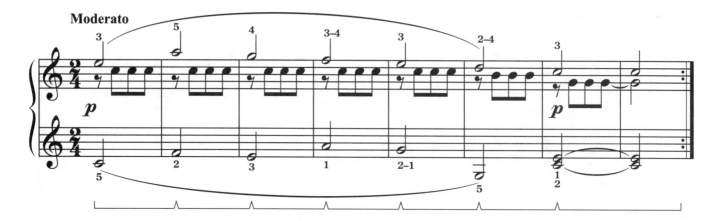

- **Blend** the repeated chords into a **murmuring background** for the LH motives. Allow the keys to push the fingers up, to **ride the keys** up and down.

- Keep the left upper arm and elbow relaxed when crossing over.

Expressive Etude
(Excerpt)

Cornelius Gurlitt (1820–1901)
Op. 51, No. 3

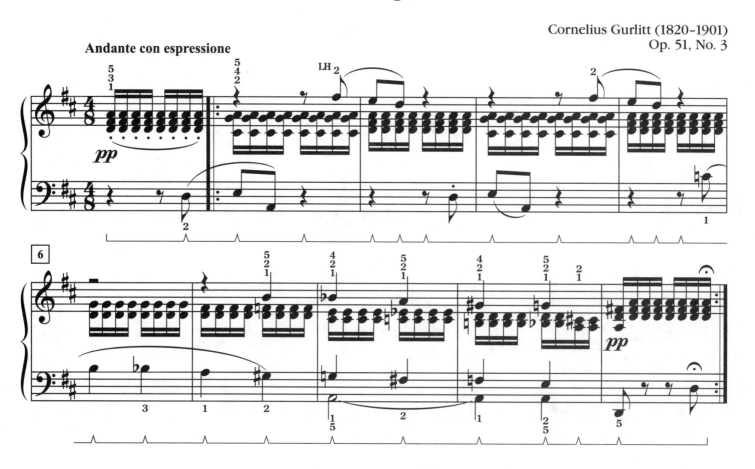

Arpeggios Divided between the Hands

The **change of hands should not be heard** when arpeggios are divided between them.

■ Make **one long line** moving to the top, turning around, and going back down.

■ **Listen carefully** to make a **perfect connection** between the thumbs (finger 1) in both hands.

Arpeggio Etude

Allegro moderato

Cornelius Gurlitt (1820–1901)
Op. 82, No. 64

Three-Quarter Blues, p. 28

Voicing: Four Voices

■ Play the half notes with a **seamless legato**, feeling and hearing a continuous connection.

■ Play the repeated eighth notes **very lightly**, keeping the weight on the half notes.

Etude in Four Voices

Jean-Baptiste Duvernoy (1802–1880)
Op. 176, No. 20

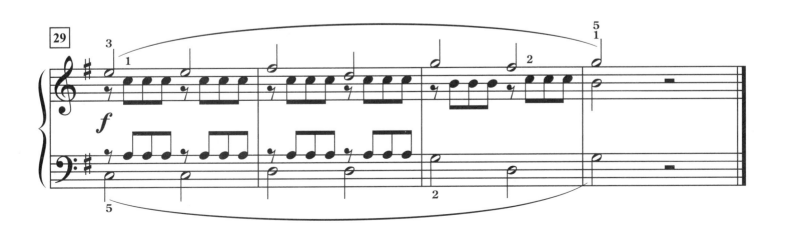

Warm-Up Patterns in A

Using a metronome to maintain a steady ♩ pulse:

■ Play the Parallel Motion scale first ♩ one octave, then ♫ two octaves, then ♫♪ three octaves, and then ♬ four octaves.

A Major Scales in Progressive Rhythms

Parallel Motion

■ Play the Combined Parallel and Contrary Motion scale as written.

Combined Parallel and Contrary Motion

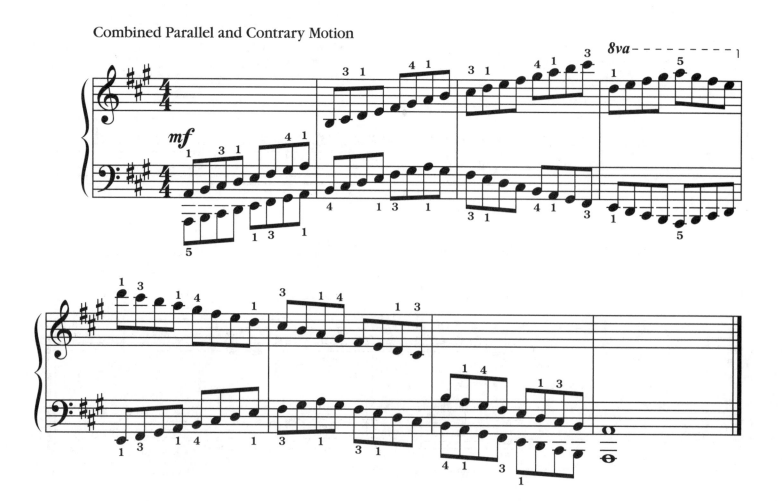

Chord Progression and Variations in A

■ Play the *Chord Progression and Variations in A* as written in major, and repeat in minor by lowering all C's and F's a half step.

■ **Relax** the wrist and knuckles after striking each chord, keeping the nail joints firm.

Blocked chord

■ **Balance** on the half notes, keeping the weight constant.

Divided chord

■ Maintain the **arch** connection between fingers 1 and 4 or 5.

Alberti bass

■ Use a **throwing motion** to group four eighth notes in one forward motion.

Divided chord pattern

Dominant Seventh Chords in A (Broken and Blocked)

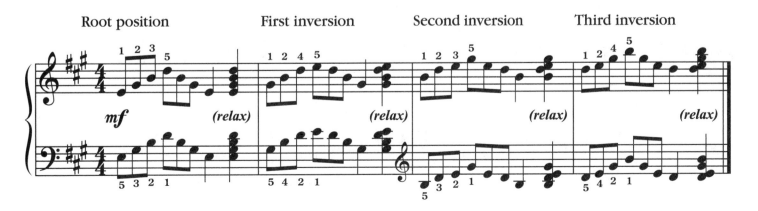

Repeat in minor by lowering all C's a half step.

Broken Chords and Inversions

- First play hands separately in ♩ rhythm. Repeat as written in ♫ rhythm.

- Align the forearm with finger 3 to begin. Lightly touch the elbow (with other hand) to keep it stationery, allowing the **wrist to pivot** as the **forearm aligns** with the finger that is playing.

Arpeggio Prep

- Keep the **hand shape** and arch between fingers 1 and 2 when crossing under the hand.

- Do not let finger 1 collapse or the hand lose its curved shape.

This

Hand shape maintained

Not This

Collapsed hand

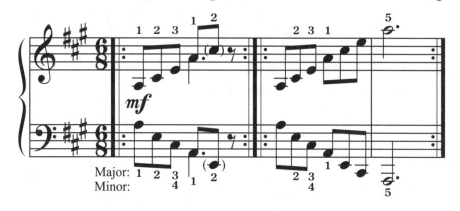

Arpeggio Exercise in A

- **Keeping the hand shape**, use a continuous forearm motion, without turning the wrist.

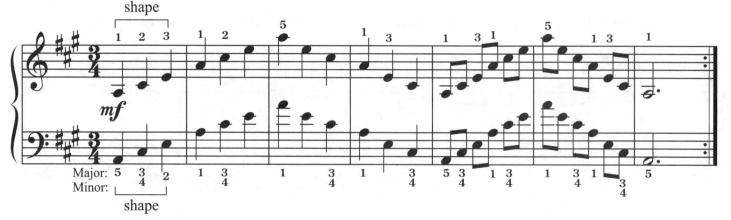

Compound Meter

Tap with both hands and count the rhythm.

$\frac{6}{8}$ is known as **compound duple meter** and is **felt in two beats per measure**.

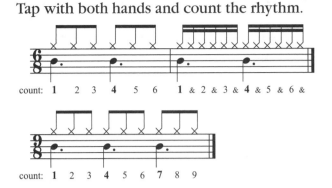

$\frac{9}{8}$ is known as **compound triple meter** and is **felt in three beats per measure**.

$\frac{12}{8}$ is known as **compound quadruple meter** and is **felt in four beats per measure**.

- **See** and **play four beats** (with **rhythmic accents**) in the measure, and show the imitation.
- Omit the mordent until the rhythm is secure.
- Add the mordent **on the beat** without disturbing the rhythm. (See page 8 for mordent exercises.)

Velocity Etude in A Major

Arnoldo Sartorio
(1853-1936)

36

The Outer Fingers (3-4-5)

The outer fingers (especially fingers 4 and 5) in each hand provide major **support** in piano playing. **Finger 5 has its own muscle** in the palm of the hand that must be activated and connected with the arms.

Finding the muscle for finger 5:

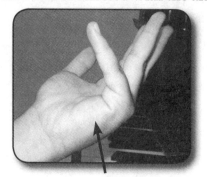

Finger 5 muscle

■ With your palm facing upward, point finger 5 to the ceiling, watching and feeling the muscle work.

■ Keeping that muscle activated, balance finger 5 on a key (supported by the forearm and triceps.)

■ Then **relax the knuckle** of finger 5, keeping the nail joint firm. Adjust the arms until comfortable.

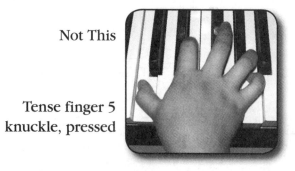

Not This

Tense finger 5
knuckle, pressed

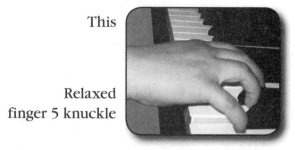

This

Relaxed
finger 5 knuckle

■ In *Voicing Etude in A Major*, balance on finger 5 (support finger), which allows the other fingers to move freely.

■ In the **double notes** such as in RH, m. 5 and LH, m. 6, first play the outer fingers alone. Keep the weight on the outer fingers when adding the inner voice. Play the four eighth notes in **one motion of the arm**.

Voicing Etude in A Major

Arnoldo Sartorio
(1853–1936)

Scale Forms in A Minor

Using a metronome to maintain a steady ♩ pulse:

■ Play each scale first ♩ one octave, then ♫ two octaves, then ♫♪ three octaves, and then ♬ four octaves.

A Minor Scales

A Natural Minor uses the key signature.

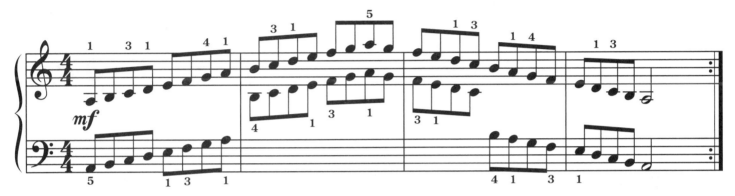

A Harmonic Minor uses the key signature with the 7th scale degree raised a half step.

A Melodic Minor uses the key signature with the 6th **and** 7th scale degrees raised a half step ascending; uses only the key signature descending (the natural minor scale).

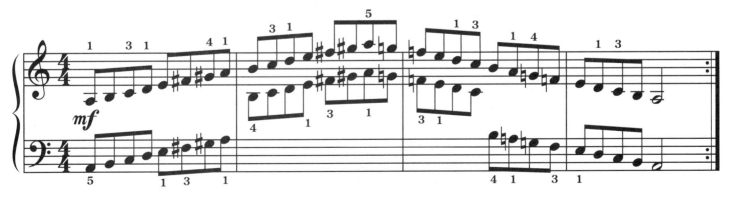

38

Melody and Repeated Chords (One Hand)

When the fingers have different tasks, it is good to practice **voices alone, hands separately**.

■ Play the **melodic line** (♩ and ♪ notes) **legato**, substituting fingers for legato connections.

■ Fingers 4 and 5 should rest **on the keys** when not playing.

■ Group the **repeated chords rhythmically** with a forward motion of the wrist and arm.

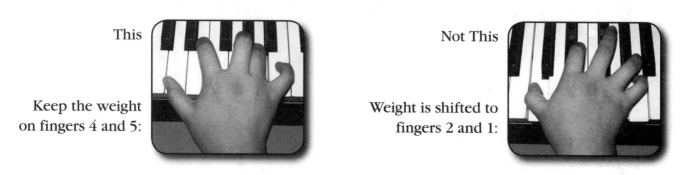

This

Keep the weight
on fingers 4 and 5:

Not This

Weight is shifted to
fingers 2 and 1:

Also play *Divided Hand Etude* with the LH one octave lower than written.

Divided Hand Etude

Jean Louis Streabbog (1835–1886)
Op. 63, No. 10

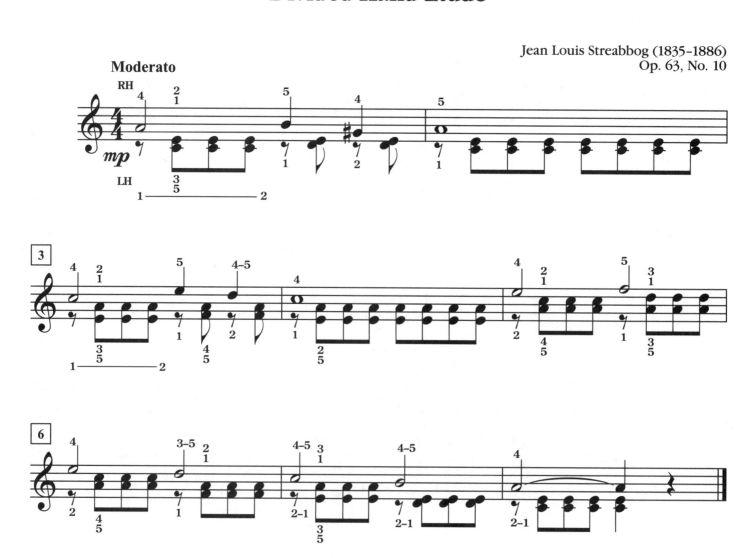

Warm-Up Patterns in F

Using a metronome to maintain a steady ♩ pulse:

■ Play the Parallel Motion scale first ♩ one octave, then ♫ two octaves, then ♪♪♪ three octaves, and then ♬♬ four octaves.

F Major Scales in Progressive Rhythms

Parallel Motion

■ Play the Combined Parallel and Contrary Motion scale as written.

Combined Parallel and Contrary Motion

Chord Progression and Variations in F

- Play the *Chord Progression and Variations in F* as written in major, and repeat in minor by lowering all A's and D's a half step.

- **Relax** the wrist and knuckles after striking each chord, keeping the nail joints firm.

Blocked chord

- **Balance** on the half notes, keeping the weight constant.

Divided chord

- Maintain the **arch** connection between fingers 1 and 4 or 5.

Alberti bass

- Use a **throwing motion** to group four eighth notes in one forward motion.

Divided chord pattern

Dominant Seventh Chords in F (Broken and Blocked)

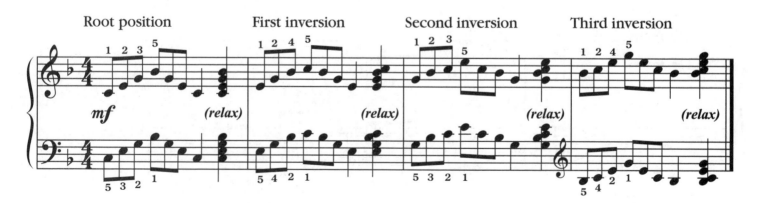

Repeat in minor by lowering all A's a half step.

Broken Chords and Inversions

■ First play hands separately in ♩ rhythm. Repeat as written in ♫ rhythm.

■ Align the forearm with finger 3 to begin. Lightly touch the elbow (with other hand) to keep it stationery, allowing the **wrist to pivot** as the **forearm aligns** with the finger that is playing.

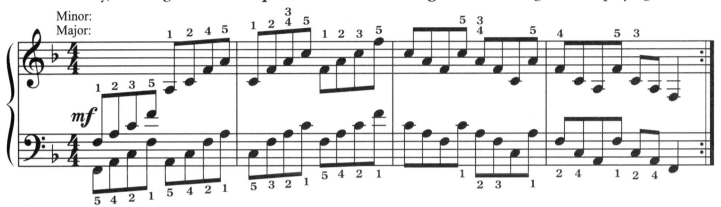

Arpeggio Prep

■ **Keeping the hand shape**, use a continuous forearm motion, without turning the wrist.

■ Repeat in minor by lowering all A's a half step.

This

Hand in position (RH)

Not This

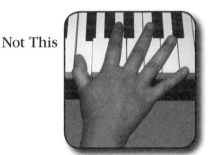

Fingers reaching for notes (RH)

Arpeggio Exercise in F

■ **Keeping the hand shape**, use a continuous forearm motion, without turning the wrist.

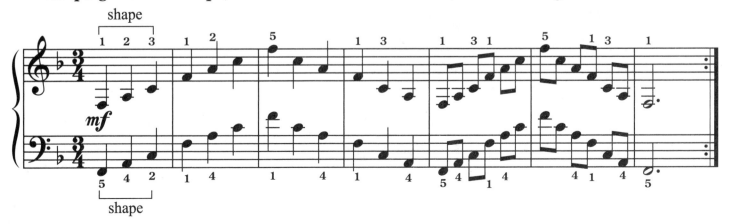

Alberti Bass Plus

The LH of *Etude in F Major* has an Alberti bass pattern and the RH has slur groups. When the hands have **different touches**, it is best to **practice them separately**.

Practice Plan:

- First, practice the Alberti bass using **the half notes to balance and support the LH**.

- To play it *p*, bring the palm close to the keyboard and play more on the **fingertips**.

- Next, practice the RH two- and three-note slurs (**fall—connect—release**).

- To produce a **full, rich melodic line**, play the RH more on the
  cushion of flesh (the pad of the finger), not the tip.

Etude in F Major is one **complete musical sentence**:

- The RH of the first two measures is a motive, slightly altered in the next two measures, making a **musical question**.

- The final four measures complete the sentence, making a **musical answer**.

Etude in F Major
(Excerpt)

Carl Czerny (1791–1857)
Op. 139, No. 23

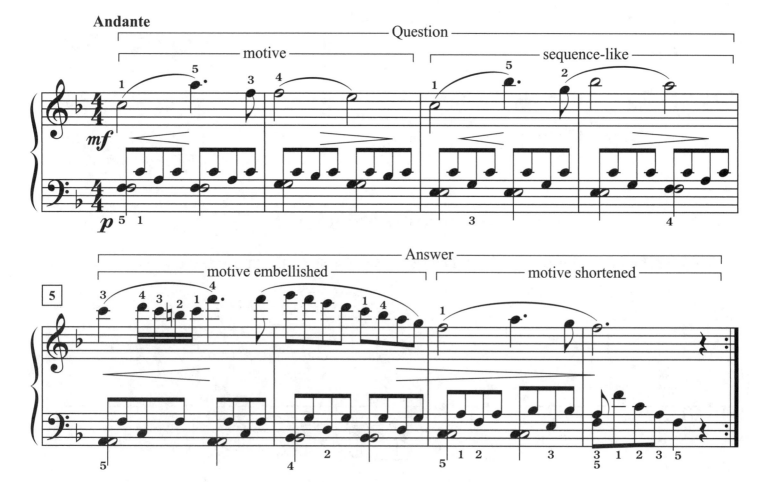

Warm-Up Patterns in B-flat

Using a metronome to maintain a steady ♩ pulse:

■ Play the Parallel Motion scale first ♩ one octave, then ♫ two octaves, then ♫♩ three octaves, and then ♬ four octaves.

B-flat Major Scale in Progressive Rhythms

Parallel Motion

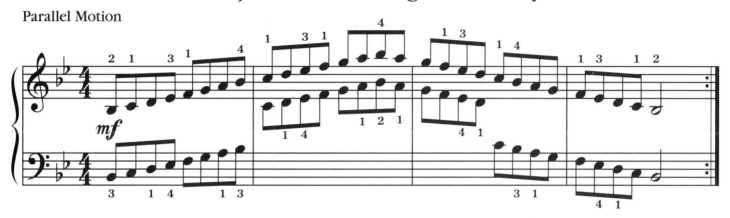

Chord Progression and Variations in B-flat

Blocked chord

■ **Balance** on the half notes, keeping the weight constant.

Divided chord

■ Maintain the **arch** connection between fingers 1 and 4 or 5.

Alberti bass

■ Use **rotation** to group four eighth notes in one forward motion.

Divided chord pattern

Dominant Seventh Chords in B-flat (Broken and Blocked)

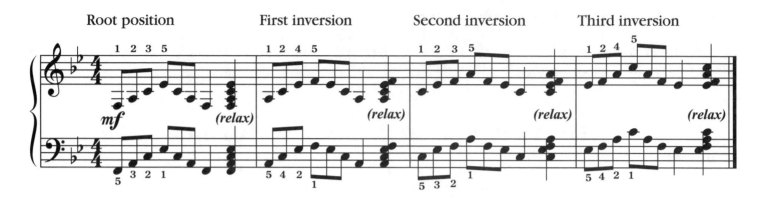

Repeat in minor by lowering all D's a half step.

Broken Chords and Inversions

■ First play hands separately in ♩ rhythm. Repeat as written in ♫ rhythm.

■ Align the forearm with finger 3 to begin. Lightly touch the elbow (with other hand) to keep it stationery, allowing the **wrist to pivot** as the **forearm aligns** with the finger that is playing.

Arpeggio Exercise in B-flat

■ **Keeping the hand shape**, use a continuous forearm motion, without turning the wrist.

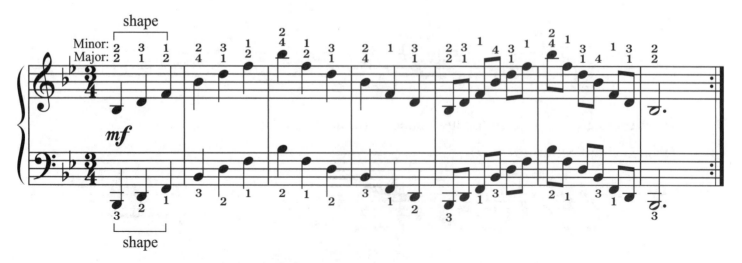

Melodious (Legato) Style

A beautiful, singing melody requires a **continuous legato touch**, with no gaps between notes.

- Legato connection is felt in the fingertips and the knuckles.

- Allow a **depressed key to rise** only when the **next key is fully depressed** by another finger.

- Listen carefully to ensure that the sound continues without break from note to note.

The arrows in the example below indicate where to lift the finger that just played the **preceding** note.

- Listen to **shape** the melodic line, letting it **grow** as it rises, and **diminish** as it falls.

- **Experiment** with tone color by playing on different parts of the fingertips.

Etude in B-flat Major
(Excerpt)

Carl Czerny (1791–1857)
Op. 823, No. 60

More about Alternating Touches

To play piano repertoire, the ability to immediately play many **different touches and dynamics** is necessary. Practice the different touches until easy and automatic.

Repeated Slur Groups:

- Each slur group is played with **one motion**. The last note is **released**, shorter than written.

- The descending slur groups (motive and sequences) should diminuendo, highlighting the scale pattern (circled).

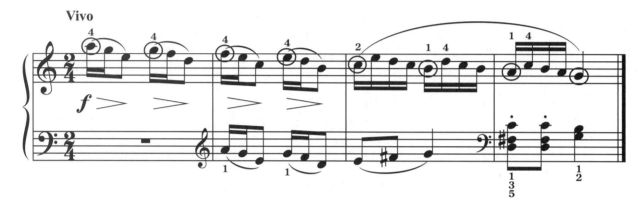

Change of Range (Large Leap):

- To arrive at the lower octave in perfect rhythm, use the **energy of the release** to carry the hand down in an **arc-like motion**.

- Group the four RH staccatos in **one motion of the arm**.

Staccato Thirds:

- Use **rotation** (similar to turning a doorknob) for the LH sixteenth notes with "angry fingers" and a relaxed arm to achieve the crescendo.

- Set the shape of the third in the RH. With very **firm fingers and a relaxed arm**, make a **knocking (or pecking) motion** from the wrist for each one.

Warm-Up Patterns in E-flat

Using a metronome to maintain a steady ♩ pulse:

■ Play the Parallel Motion scale first ♩ one octave, then ♫ two octaves, then ♫♩ three octaves, and then ♬ four octaves.

E-flat Major Scale in Progressive Rhythms

Parallel Motion

Chord Progression and Variations in E-flat

Blocked chord

■ **Fall** on the first note and **connect** with the upper arm (like a slur motion).

■ The **repeated chords** are played with one forward motion (toward the fallboard).

■ To find the chords without looking, use B-flat as placement to feel the octave. Practice the hand shifts feeling the B-flat.

Velocity (Speed) in E-flat Major

When playing scales that have several flats:

■ The thumb angle must be high enough to help **balance the fingers on the black keys**. Experiment to find arm support and balance.

■ Direct **energy** to the arch of the hand.

Etude in E-flat Major

Carl Czerny (1791–1857)
Op. 261, No. 27

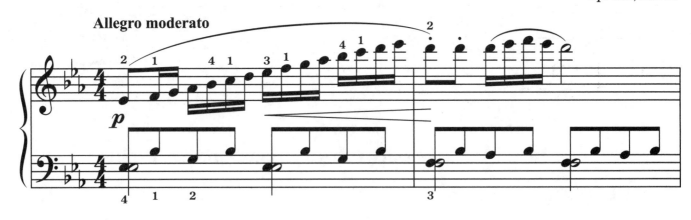

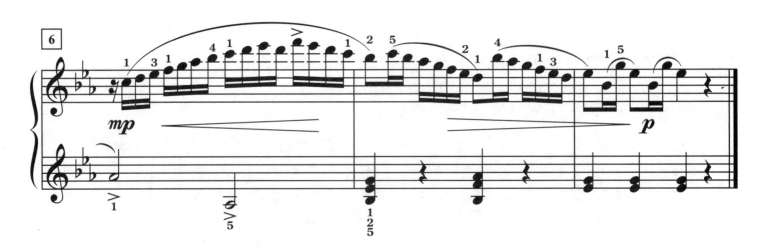

Warm-Up Patterns in E

Using a metronome to maintain a steady ♩ pulse:

■ Play the Parallel Motion scale first ♩ one octave, then ♫ two octaves, then ♫♩ three octaves, and then ♫♫ four octaves.

E Major Scales in Progressive Rhythms

Parallel Motion

■ Play the Combined Parallel and Contrary Motion scale as written.

Combined Parallel and Contrary Motion

Chord Progression and Variations in E

■ Play the *Chord Progression and Variations in E* as written in major, and repeat in minor by lowering all G's and C's a half step.

■ **Relax** the wrist and knuckles after striking each chord, keeping the nail joints firm.

Blocked chord

■ **Balance** on the half notes, keeping the weight constant.

Divided chord

■ Maintain the **arch** connection between fingers 1 and 4 or 5.

Alberti bass

■ Use a **throwing motion** to group four eighth notes in one forward motion.

Divided chord pattern

Dominant Seventh Chords in E (Broken and Blocked)

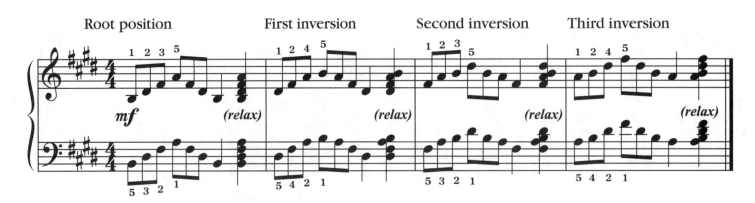

Repeat in minor by lowering all G's a half step.

Broken Chords and Inversions

- First play hands separately in ♩ rhythm. Repeat as written in ♫ rhythm.

- Align the forearm with finger 3 to begin. Lightly touch the elbow (with other hand) to keep it stationery, allowing the **wrist to pivot** as the **forearm aligns** with the finger that is playing.

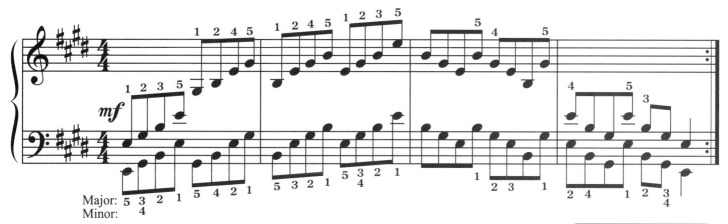

Arpeggio Prep

- **Position the hand** over the notes of the next octave after crossing the thumb under the hand.

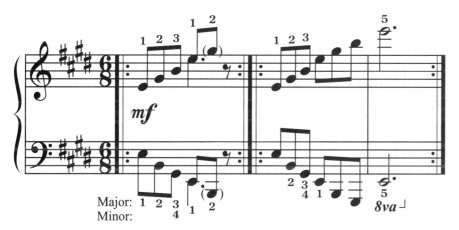

This

Hand in position (LH)

Not This

Fingers reaching for notes (LH)

Arpeggio Exercise in E

- **Keeping the hand shape**, use a continuous forearm motion, without turning the wrist.

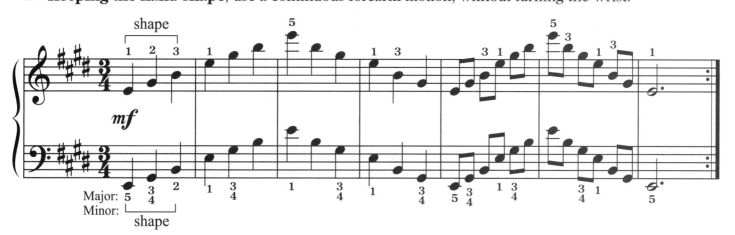

52

Minuet, p. 42

Closed and Open Hand

■ When the hand is open to the interval of a 5th or 6th, it is a **closed hand position**.

■ When playing an octave, **open the palm** (from the knuckle of finger 5 to the first joint of finger 1) comfortably to the larger interval.

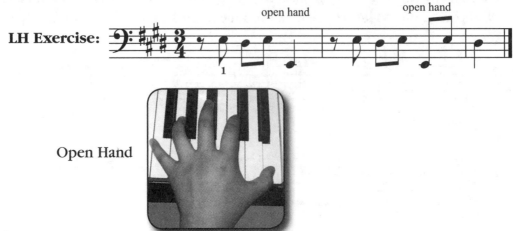

Open Hand

Divided Hand

Keep constant weight on the outer fingers, allowing **gravity** to hold the fingers on the keys.

■ **Listen** to hear the **different tone colors** in the inner and outer voices.

■ Play each measure in **one motion** (like a slur group.)

Etude in E Major

Carl Czerny (1791–1857)
Op. 261, No. 49

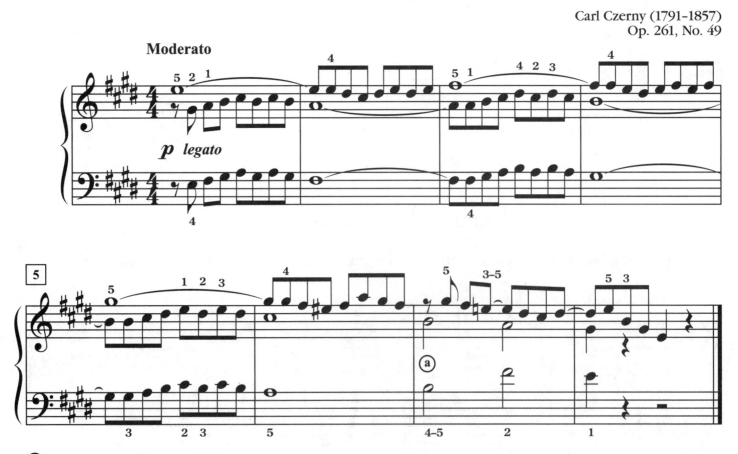

ⓐ The editor simplified m. 7 slightly.

Scale Forms in E Minor

Using a metronome to maintain a steady ♩ pulse:

■ Play each scale first ♩ one octave, then ♫ two octaves, then ⌐♩♩♩ three octaves, and then ♬♬ four octaves.

E Minor Scales

E Natural Minor uses the key signature.

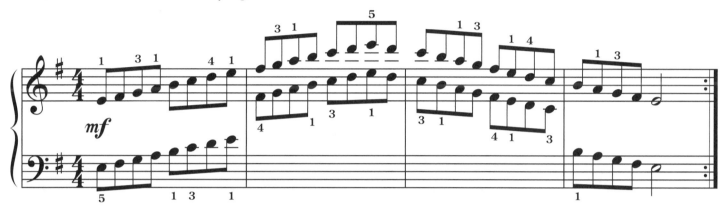

E Harmonic Minor uses the key signature with the 7th scale degree raised a half step.

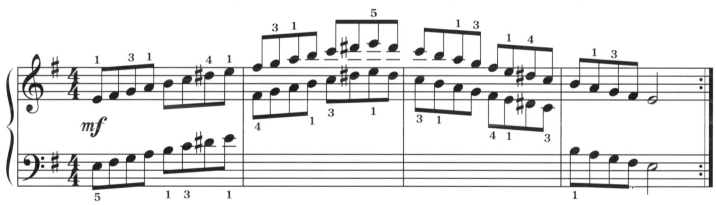

E Melodic Minor uses the key signature with the 6th **and** 7th scale degrees raised a half step ascending; uses only the key signature descending (the natural minor scale).

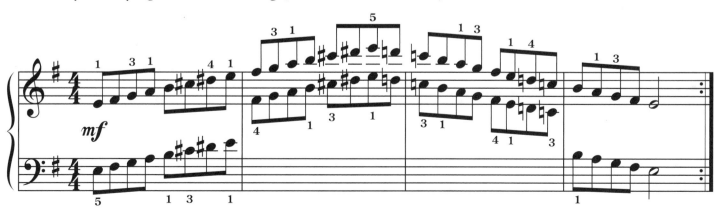

Left-Hand Velocity

Speed in passagework comes from playing **many notes in one arm motion**, like a long slur group.

■ With the left wrist suspended, as it falls to level, allow the **weight to flow through the wrist** to firm nail joints.

■ Feeling **one group for each measure**, give the first note of each measure (or when changing direction) a **faster finger stroke** for momentum.

■ **Align** the forearm with each finger as it plays.

Left-Hand Etude

Louis Köhler
(1820–1886)

More Voicing: Four Parts

■ Using the whole and half notes as support finger frees the others. First play the longer notes alone, then move the other fingers to feel this.

■ Play the slur groups in one arm motion. Relax the forearm into the finger nail joints.

Running with Four Voices
(Excerpt)

Carl Czerny (1791–1857)
Op. 139, No. 43
Arr. Nancy Bachus

Dance of the Gnomes, p. 48

Grouping Staccatos

Before playing *Scherzando* (below), play the LH line with two hands. Allow energy to flow through the wrists and knuckles to the fingertips.

- When playing as written in *Scherzando*, bring out the descending line in the LH.

- Keep the weight in the outer fingers.

Weight in
outer hand

To play continuous staccato lines:

- First, play the lines **legato** with the RH as three-note slurs (except mm. 11–12).

- Next, play with a **fingertip staccato**, keeping the fingers **on the keys**.

- Feel **one motion of the arm** for each measure.

Scherzando

Cornelius Gurlitt (1820–1901)
Op. 141, No. 18